Hope of Heaven

Expectations and Descriptions

Hope of Heaven: Expectations and Descriptions
Copyright © 2006 by James Byers
ISBN-10   0-9822618-7-X
ISBN-13   978-0-9822618-7-3
Portions edited by:
Rosemary J. Hilliard, Jennifer Lowry, and Annalisa Mann
Cover design by Whitnee Webb
Book Block design by Whitnee Webb
All rights reserved. No part of this publication may be reproduced or transmitted in any form or by any means without written permission of the author.
Published by:
O'More Publishing
A Division of O'More College of Design
423 South Margin St.
Franklin, TN 37064 U.S.A

Hope of Heaven

Expectations and Descriptions

James Byers

O'MORE
PUBLISHING

Content

Part One: Expectations
Lord Come Quickly
A Study of the Parousia in the New Testament

Introduction	1
1. The Gospel Writers	3
2. The Book of Acts	9
3. The Letters of Paul	13
4. Hebrews and James	21
5. Apocalyptic Writings	27
6. Summary	35
Selected Sources	38
End Notes	40

Part Two: Descriptions
Heavenly Words
Descriptions of Heaven in the New Testament

7. Foreshadows of Heaven	45
8. The Kingdom of Heaven	49
9. The Heavenly House of God	53
10. A Heavenly Paradise	57
11. Heavenly Citizenship	63
12. A Heavenly Country	69
13. The Shaking of the Heavens	75
14. The Heavenly Body	79
15. Heavenly Visions	87
16. The Church Enrolled in Heaven	93
17. The Heavenly Sabbath Rest	99
18. Final Thoughts about Heaven	103
Selected Sources	108
End Notes	112

Part One: Expectations

Lord Come Quickly

A Study of ***Parousia*** in the New Testament

Introduction

In First Corinthians 16:22, the apostle Paul made an unusual plea. The words used in that plea, *Maran-atha*, are Aramaic in origin and can be translated several ways. The first division of the words would imply that the Lord has come. *Maran-atha* could also indicate a plea to come or that the Lord is coming.

The passage has become a key scripture for those in modern times who expect the immediate return of the Lord. These people sometimes conclude prayers with such a plea. This begs the question: does the New Testament specifically point to an eminent, even hasty, return of Jesus Christ? What did Jesus say about His return? The New Testament itself provides many of the answers.

Chapter One

The Gospel Writers

The Gospel of Matthew contains the most complete picture of the *parousia*, the return coming of Christ. The people of Jesus' time put great value in unusual signs occurring outside the realm of nature. In Matthew 24:3, the disciples asked Jesus on the Mount of Olives about the sign of His second coming or *parousia*. His own disciples saw the *parousia* as the final event of the "completion of the age."

Jesus used "completion of the age" in Matthew 28:20 when He told His disciples that He would be with them to the end of the age. This was reassuring as He had just given them the commission to save the planet in verse nineteen. The writer of Hebrews also used this expression in Hebrews 9:26–27 when he talked about the sacrifice of Jesus that occurred at the end of the ages. This writer added that, according to God's plan, human beings die, and then there is a final judgment.

Thus, end of the age or ages can mean several things. However, in Matthew 24 the reference was specifically pointing to a return visit by Jesus. Matthew 24 has been traditionally divided into two separate events which Jesus explained in great detail. There will be an end to the Jewish age culminating in the destruction of the temple in 70 A.D. The second part of the division centers on the coming of Jesus as Christ from heaven. Alfred Plummer, a British commentator, believed that many in Jesus' day would regard the destruction of Jerusalem as "the end of the World." The word immediately *(eutheos)*, which may also be translated directly or straightway, has lead us to believe that Matthew expected a speedy *parousia*. Paul used the word immediately in Galatians 1:16 to refer to the next event after his conversion. No exact time period for this event in Galatians is documented. [1]

From both verses we can conclude that less than an exact period of time was indicated in Matthew 24 after the fall of Jerusalem, but that the next significant event after the fall was to be the final appearance of Christ. Plummer concluded, "The end will not come until the Gospel has been preached to all nations, and that the End will be preceded by a variety of religious, political, and physical disturbances." The distinguished scholar J.W. McGarvey added the comment that if we translate *eutheos* as immediately then "we must consider Peter's analysis of time in regards to God i.e. a thousand years is as a day." Matthew seemed to emphasize the division of these events even more when he stated that the day and hour no one knows except the Father. Jesus and the angels were excluded from such knowledge, at least while the earthly ministry took place. Yet, Jesus will be the one coming. This coming will be in power and glory, and Jesus will be accompanied by angels who will gather the chosen ones. [2]

In a similar fashion to other New Testament writers, Matthew set a high standard for the explanation of the coming of Christ by using the word *parousia*, the final coming, instead of the word rapture or second coming. Moreover, in Matthew the emphasis is on the ideas of surprise and preparation. Jesus told the story of Noah, of the diligent servant, of the wise bridesmaids, and of those people who use their talents wisely. The people of Noah's day ate and drank and did not change their lives. The servant was doing the work of his Lord while the Lord was absent. The wise bridesmaids were ready to light their lamps even though the bridegroom did not return on the expected schedule. The wise men used their talents and did not neglect their investment while their Lord was away.

Matthew focused on preparation for the *parousia*, not in a bizarre or extraordinary way, but by constant attention to daily tasks. He was not concerned with the time of the *parousia*, and, as mentioned, Matthew even indicated that while on earth Jesus was not privy to the time. Certainly Matthew did not provide the complete answer to the statement, "Lord come quickly." He did tell us what we ought to know. There will be a coming of Christ that will be in power. The coming will not be expected as the stories in chapters 24 and 25 indicate. All believers should be prepared for this coming. As Plummer saw it, "The lesson from Noah and his generation is that those who heed God's warnings are delivered, while those who refuse to do so are left to their fate." [3]

Of all the Gospel writers, Matthew connected the *parousia* to the judgment of humanity. His gospel mentioned judgment many times. In Matthew 11:21, Jesus pronounced judgment upon the cities of Chorazin and Bethsaida. Matthew used the words *hemera kriseos*, the day of judgment. In chapter 12:41 Nineveh, which repented, will rise up in judgement, *krisei*. In verse 42 of the same chapter, the Queen of the South will be raised in the judgment and will literally judge against *katakrinei*, those who did not honor Jesus. For this gospel writer, *parousia's* meaning included judgment. Jesus was pictured as the glorified Lord accompanied by His angels. He will separate and judge the peoples of the earth. Judgment will be based upon seemingly insignificant matters: feeding the hungry, clothing the unclothed, providing drink for the thirsty, visiting those in prison. Other issues including doctrinal teachings were not mentioned. The *parousia* reached climax with the judgment scene.

The Gospel of John is a different kind of gospel. This gospel also approached the *parousia* in a different way. John did not use the word *parousia* in his gospel and only once in his letters. In I John 2:28, he exhorted his children to abide in Christ that they may have confidence not to be ashamed before Him at His coming (*parousia*). In John's gospel the wording was different. In John 5:22, he wrote about judgment that was assigned to the Son. In John 5:28–29, Jesus told His listeners about the resurrection of those who have done good, who will be raised to life, and those who have done evil to the resurrection of judgment. In John 12:48, Jesus referred to judgment as the last day using similar language as Matthew (*esxate hemera*).

These expressions signified in John's mind a *parousia* or coming again. Two of these passages buttress the idea of judgment which Matthew emphasized repeatedly. John used the words coming again in a similar fashion as Matthew uses *parousia*. Both writers referred to an event that will end earthly history and will involve a final judgment. The words *last day* were recorded by John to indicate this coming again and are similar in meaning to Matthew's words that he described as the day of judgment.

Chapter Two
The Book of Acts

The Book of Acts has been described as a selective history of the early church. The book includes examples of conversion, sermons, trials, and travel. The word *parousia* was not used by the writer Luke, but he recorded at least three sermons that concentrate on this concept.

The first sermon was delivered by Peter at Solomon's porch following the healing of a crippled man. In this sermon Peter reached a climax where he said, "Repent therefore and be converted, that your sins may be blotted out so that times of refreshing may come from the presence of the Lord, and that He may send Jesus Christ, who was preached to you before, whom heaven must receive until the times of restoration of all things, which God has spoken by the mouth of all His holy prophets since the world began" (Acts 3:19-21). Peter describes the *parousia* as a restoration (*apokatastaseos*). As the writer R. E. Rackham interpreted, "And the times for this restoration would come when Jesus, as a second Elijah, returned from heaven." Peter did not completely clarify what this restoration includes, but from all indications, restoration in the New Testament proposes that the final restoring will occur at the coming or the *parousia* of Jesus Christ. [4]

In Acts, Paul was more specific as to the *parousia* when he preached in Athens on the Areopagus. In Acts 17: 30–31, he told the assembled Athenians, "Truly, these times of ignorance God overlooked, but now commands all men everywhere to repent, because He has appointed a day on which He will judge the world in righteousness by the Man whom He has ordained. He has given assurance of this to all by raising Him from the dead." Paul was here referring to a day of judgment as Matthew and John did. As Rackham stated, "Creation itself, as it is, involves a day of judgment, when God's purpose shall be fulfilled and order restored to the universe. This day was eternally appointed in the divine will, and has its place in the appointed seasons." [5]

The idea of judgment did not scandalize the Athenians as much as the idea of the resurrected body. The Greeks believed in some kind of afterlife, but, even in the best of circumstances, the afterlife did not favorably compare with earthly life. The Jewish people, on the other hand, had a slightly more optimistic view of the hereafter. Martha, a friend of Jesus, believed in a final resurrection when contemplating the death of her beloved brother Lazarus (John 11).

In Acts 24:24–25, Paul made a defense of the gospel before Felix, the Governor of Judea: "And after some days, when Felix came with his wife Drusilla, who was Jewish, he sent for Paul and heard him concerning the faith in Christ. Now as he reasoned about righteousness, self control, and the judgment to come, Felix was afraid and answered, 'Go away for now; when I have a convenient time I will call for you.'" The word Paul used for judgment involved the meaning of a legal process, the same as he was undergoing before Felix. It is the same word used by Jesus in condemning the Pharisees for their hypocrisy (Matthew 23:13). Even a Roman governor understood the consequences of conduct, and Paul must have presented his argument well. We can only imagine the thoughts of Felix. He was deeply troubled, and the coming of judgment sobered him, as it must any reasonable person.

Chapter Three

The Letters of Paul

Certain letters of Paul concentrated on the *parousia*. Other letters did not mention it. With Paul the *parousia* was always discussed when someone or some assembly was confused or completely incorrect about the meaning of the word. The letters that discuss in detail the word *parousia* are Corinthians, Thessalonians, Philippians, and Timothy. Certain letters of Paul did refer to a judgment day. Paul wrote in Romans 2:5–8: "But in accordance with your hardness and your impenitent heart, you are treasuring up for yourself wrath in the day of wrath and revelation of the righteous judgment of God. Who will render to each one according to his deeds, eternal life to those who by patient continuance in doing good seek for glory, honor, and immortality; but to those who are self seeking and do not obey the truth, but obey unrighteousness, indignation, and wrath."

In this passage Paul anticipated a day of wrath that will also be a day of revelation. The final day will be the day of God's anger, just as Jesus showed anger against the Pharisees in Mark 3:5 when they disapproved of His healing a man on the Sabbath. This type of anger referred to a disposition that God will manifest at the last day. The observation was made by Paul that in the judgment the anger would be administered by Christ, certainly a new concept to Jewish readers of the letter. Paul also referred to an apocalyptic vision of the judgment day, the *apokalupsis*. Revelation and judgment will occur on the day of wrath.

In the letters to the Corinthians, the *parousia* discussion was much more detailed. Paul delineated the chronology of the *parousia* in chapter 15 of First Corinthians. The church in the city of Corinth was greatly baffled by the issues of the coming of Jesus as well as the resurrection of the body. Paul, as he did in Athens, explained that resurrection will occur at the time of the *parousia*. A basic point of discussion in chapter 15 was the problem of the resurrection. Imbedded in Greek thought was the concept of the spirit forever separated from the body. Paul taught them that the resurrection of a celestial body is essential to the Christian faith.

In chapter 15:51–55, Paul wrote, "Behold, I tell you a mystery: we shall not all sleep, but we shall all be changed in a moment, in the twinkling of an eye, at the last trumpet. For the trumpet will sound and the dead will be raised incorruptible, and we shall be changed. For this corruptible must put on incorruption, and this mortal must put on immortality. So when this corruptible has put on incorruption and this mortal has put on immortality, then shall be brought to pass the saying that is written: 'Death is swallowed up in victory. O Death where is your sting? Hades where is your victory?'"

With Paul the *parousia* had become a victory song, a triumph beyond compare. The *parousia* will be accompanied by transformation. Those who were dead will be resurrected in celestial bodies; those who are alive will be transformed into celestial bodies. Therefore, the coming was compared to a transformation (*allasso*). Paul used the word to indicate a great change as he did in Romans 1:23 when the Gentiles changed, or transformed, God into corruptible idols. In this chapter the emphasis was on believers. Judgment was not discussed. Victory was assured to the believer. Paul believed that victory was near. As Robertson and Plummer in their commentary stated, "But the belief that the advent is near would seem to have been constant. Evidently the apostle had no idea of centuries of interval before the Advent." That Paul and others were disappointed may explain First

Corinthians 16:22, "O Lord, come." The expectation was there. The hope has continued through the centuries. [6]

In the second letter to the Corinthians, Paul was no less confident of the coming (*parousia*) of Christ. He was very wary of offering immediate expectation, rather relying on the promise of transformation. In Second Corinthians 5: 1–4, he wrote, "For we know that if our earthly house, this tent (*skenous*), is destroyed, we have a building from God, a house not made with hands, eternal in the heavens. For in this we groan, earnestly desiring to be clothed with our habitation which is from heaven, if indeed, having been clothed, we shall not be found naked. For we who are in this tent groan, being burdened, not because we want to be unclothed, but further clothed, that mortality may be swallowed up by life." In verse 10 he concluded, "For we must all appear before the judgment seat of Christ, that each one may receive the things done in the body, according to what he has done whether good or bad."

Here, Paul defined the *parousia* as both a judgment and a transformation. He had not emphasized judgment in First Corinthians 15, rather the celestial body being resurrected. In Second Corinthians he added judgment as part of the future coming. The judgment seat (*bema*) was the official place of judgment in Roman society. Paul had been present at the *bema* in Corinth (Acts 18:12) before the judge,

Gallio, Proconsul of Achaia. Paul's case was dismissed by Gallio on that occasion, and perhaps Paul was reminded of this word in writing to the Corinthians. His point was clear: conduct does matter.

In the transformation passage of First Corinthians 15, Paul concluded that the *parousia* was a time of great change. We will be transformed from an earthly dwelling to the heavenly abode. Our spiritual transformation will include a celestial body. In Second Corinthians, the *parousia* was both judgment and release. The mortal will become immortal. The weariness and burden will be gone. When this shall happen is still not certain as to time.

A sister Greek fellowship to Corinth was in the northern city of Thessalonika. In this city *parousia* fever reached new heights. The Thessalonian Christians were not only concerned with the resurrected body, but they were very concerned with the exact time of the *parousia*. This concern included the time of the *parousia*, the order of ascent into heaven, and if any one would be left behind. In First Thessalonians 4:13–18, Paul addressed their concern for those of their number already deceased. He told these Christians that their loved ones will have preference and priority at the *parousia*: "We who are alive and remain until the coming of the Lord will by no means precede those who are asleep." The word that we translate as precede is taken from the root word *phthano* and means to come before or anticipate. In several passages in the New Testament, the word simply meant to attain. Paul was telling the Thessalonians that the living will not attain the eternal prize before the deceased. Paul used a word, *koimao*, which literally meant to be asleep. In Acts 12:6, the word described Peter's sleeping in his prison cell. For Jesus and Paul, the word was a euphemism for death. An example from Jesus would be His description of Lazarus sleeping (John 11:11).

The Thessalonian church had most likely experienced deaths in its fellowship. Paul then used this sorrow to describe the *parousia* in terms of comfort. First Thessalonians 4:16 stated the Lord will summon all to meet their Lord. J.B. Lightfoot in his commentary stated, "There is nothing more certain than that the New Testament represents the general judgment of mankind as ushered in by an actual visible appearance of our Lord on earth. And the announcement of the angels is not more explicit on this point than the universal language of the New Testament." [7]

Apparently, the problems of the *parousia* had not completely disappeared with the Thessalonians when Paul wrote his second letter to them. The emphasis then shifted from who will enjoy the *parousia* benefits to when this event would happen and the accompanying responsibilities, if any, in anticipation of the *parousia*. With such a frenzied attitude on the part of the Thessalonians, Paul had to soothe frayed nerves. First of all he addressed the "man of sin" in the second chapter of the letter. Numerous identifications about this man have been attempted for many years, from Caligula, Nero, or Domitian in ancient times to modern despots in Europe, the Middle East, or other parts of the world. The rulers of the world come and go, and one must concede, as Rollin Walker commented, "It is always true in every battle for good that the Son of Man does not come until the falling away comes and the man of sin is revealed. It is exceedingly important that men should be delivered from shallow optimism." [8]

Paul's answer to such frenetic hope was quiet labor. The suggestion was very strong that the Thessalonians were waiting for the day of Christ and were neglecting everyday affairs of life, becoming idle and disorderly. The lesson of Second Thessalonians is that the day of Christ will be preceded by the "man of sin" (*anthropos hamartias*). The process of *parousia* has begun and will be concluded according to God's time. Meanwhile Christians were to live lives in quietness while not growing weary in well doing.

After confronting the excessive anticipation of the Thessalonians concerning the *parousia*, Paul continued to deal with matters of the second coming. The Corinthians had problems with a bodily resurrection as did many other Greeks. Paul was never deterred from a positive expectation of the *parousia*. In Philippians he wrote, "Our citizenship is in heaven, from which we also eagerly wait for the savior, the Lord Jesus Christ" (Philippians 3:20). In later years when Paul was in prison for the last time, some Christians had either given up or were teaching a secret resurrection. Paul confronted the second heresy in his second letter to Timothy. He talks about false teachers who spread heresies like gangrene and confronted Hymenaeus and Philetus "who have strayed concerning the truth, saying the resurrection is already past: and they overthrow the faith of some" (II Timothy 2:17–18). Paul used the familiar phrase "missing the mark" (*astaxeo*) regarding a failure to keep the truth. This phrase was similar to the term for sin (*hamartia*) in the New Testament. Of course, such fallacies were deeply troubling to Paul.

Paul had come to terms with his own expectations concerning the *parousia*. He admitted that Christ would probably not return in his lifetime. That Day would not be seen by him on earth. Already, he saw himself going to be with the Lord (Philippians 1:23). He wrote to Timothy that he was being "poured out" and the time of his departure (*analuseos*) was at hand. He was confident that the Day would come, and all who love his appearing would be rewarded.

Chapter Four

Hebrews and James

In the Biblical canon two letters, Hebrews and James, have been positioned between the Pauline epistles and the so-called apocalyptic letters of Peter, Jude, and John. The Book of Hebrews has remained a mystery as to authorship. The date of authorship seems to be a generation removed from the life of Christ. The audience was Hebrew Christians who were greatly distressed. The expectation of a triumphant return of Christ had not been fulfilled. The writer of Hebrews attempted to assure his readers with such expressions as "in these last days" (Hebrews 1:2). He followed with promises such as "for we who have believed do enter that rest" (Hebrews 4:3) and "there remains therefore a rest for the people of God" (Hebrews 4:9).

The *parousia* was brought into play in Hebrews 9:27–28: "And it is appointed for man to die once, but after this the judgment. So Christ was offered once to bear the sins of many. To those who eagerly await for Him He will appear a second time, apart from sin for salvation." The great writer B.F. Westcott commented, "In this case the complete acceptance of Christ's work by the Father testified by the return in glory, is the correlative to the sentence given on human life. He rises above judgment, and yet His absolute righteousness receives this testimony. For Him what is judgment in the case of men is seen in the return to bear the final message of salvation." [9]

The writer of Hebrews continued the thoughts of judgment when he wrote, "And let us hold fast the confession of our hope without wavering, for He who promised is faithful. And let us consider one another in order to stir up love and good works not forsaking the assembly of ourselves together, as the manner of some, but exhorting one another, and so much more as you see the day approaching. For if we sin willingly after we have received the knowledge of the truth, there no longer remains a sacrifice for sins, but a certain fearful expectation of judgment, and fiery indignation which will devour the adversaries" (Hebrews 10: 24–27). Concerning the Lord's speedy return, Westcott observed that this concept "is found expressed in each group of writings of the N.T. and under the same term *parousia*." [10]

In chapter eleven, the writer of Hebrews talked of the heavenly country: "But now they desire a better, that is a heavenly country" (Hebrews 11:16). In chapter twelve he exhorted the listeners: "But you have come to Mount Zion and to the city of the living God, the heavenly Jerusalem, to an innumerable company of angels, to the general assembly and church of the firstborn who are registered in heaven, to God the judge of all and to spirits of just people made perfect" (Hebrews 12: 22, 23). Westcott stated, "These are angels and men, no longer separated, as at Sinai, by signs of great terror, but united in one vast assembly." [11]

The writer of Hebrews has elevated the benefits of the promised *parousia*. The children of God will come to His Mountain, to the city of the living Deity, to the heavenly Jerusalem. They will be with countless angels in a festival assembly (*panegursis*), and with the church (*ekklesia*) of the first born ones. Although *parousia* as a word was not used in Hebrews, the glorious coming of Christ was promised everywhere. The great day was approaching. There would be impending judgment. The heavenly country was awaiting those who searched for the city whose builder was God. This city was the heavenly Jerusalem, and the angels were there to greet the saints. The church of the first born ones would be there with the names written in the register. God the Judge will be there with the spirits of those who have been perfected.

The recipients of this letter were encouraged because the writer told them heavenly help would come in the final days. That final day will come even though saints have given up, but the Book of Hebrews says never lose hope. God will come, and the heavenly city will be prepared. The glorious assembly of heavenly beings will be waiting. Life on earth will not be the end. Christians must eagerly wait for the coming of the Lord.

When we examine James, we examine a letter with a strong Jewish background. James was thought to be the half brother of Jesus, and one who came to his belief in Jesus only after the resurrection. James then became the leader of the Jerusalem church, presiding over the Jerusalem conference in 50 A.D. His letter has been considered the most practical in the New Testament. He was not afraid to deal with troubling issues. In particular he attacked the moral and social injustices of his age. Whether focusing on fellow Christians or non Christians, James showed no difference. He emphasized that the time for judgment was near.

In the final chapter of his short letter, he gave full attention to the coming *parousia*: "Be patient then, brethren, until the *parousia* of the Lord" (James 5:7). The commentator Lenski wrote, "It is true that the Christians of apostolic times lived in constant expectation of the *Parousia* as we all ought to live." The trouble with us is that almost 2000 years have passed, and we have come to think that the *Parousia* is still far off, though, truly, "Christians may expect it at any time." (12)

In fact, James himself saw the *parousia* as near and warned his readers about complaining: "Do not keep groaning brethren against each other in order that you may not be judged. Lo, the Judge is standing before the door!" Lenski observed, "And the readers must know that the Judge is already standing before the door. He has risen and has come near. What if he opens the door and steps in as suddenly and unexpectedly as he has said he will and finds us impatient, groaning at each other in dissatisfaction instead of being patient and firm?" (13)

James emphasized patience in waiting for the *parousia*. His examples were the farmer, the prophets of the Old Testament, and Job. All have suffered disappointment and tragedy. The *parousia* will rectify all of these sufferings. James' *parousia* was defined as the judgment where the morally corrupt and the socially uncaring will be dealt the harshest of realities. For the Christian, endurance (*hupomone*) is the key. James wrote his letter a generation after the resurrection of Christ. Christians were still either ignoring the *parousia*, or they were in a state of depression because it had not occurred. This problem continued into the apocalyptic letters of the New Testament.

Chapter Five

Apocalyptic Writings

The remaining letters of the New Testament were directed even more emphatically toward the coming of Christ, the *parousia*. These letters have sometimes been labeled the apocalyptic epistles. The *parousia* theme was especially prevalent in Second Peter. The scholar Bigg wrote, "Throughout the epistle great stress is laid upon fear and the thought of the Day of Judgment. For him, therefore, leading thoughts are the knowledge of the Lord and the terrors of the Day of Judgment." [14]

In all likelihood the letters of Peter were written after Paul's letters to Thessalonika and Corinth. Tension in the church, even persecution, was present. The people of Asia Minor (modern-day Turkey) were having very serious doubts about the return of Jesus. In Second Peter 3:4 the question "where is the promise of His coming (*parousia*)?" would indicate great uncertainty from the Christians at that time. The doubt could have come from teachers of philosophy, or even from fellow Christians.

The intense expectation of the early return of Christ had come back to haunt the New Testament writers. Could Paul have been wrong about the time? What did Jesus really mean about His *parousia*? Was there to be a final judgment? All were good questions that needed to be answered. Peter resorted to a theoretical concept as well as a moral argument. In Second Peter 3:8–9, he commented, "But, beloved, do not forget this one thing, that with the Lord one day is as a thousand years, and a thousand years as one day. The Lord is not slack concerning His promise, as some count slackness, but is longsuffering toward us, not willing that any should perish but that all should come to repentance."

The writer Bigg agreed, he commented "what Peter wishes is to contrast the eternity of God with the impatience of human expectations. What does God mean by a day? It may be a thousand years. The Lord delays in order that all men may have time to repent and be saved." [15] Peter noted that the coming will be unexpected, echoing the sayings of Jesus. However, Peter was one of the New

Testament writers who explained that the old world will completely pass away. As John did in Revelation, Peter envisioned a new creation, a new world. The old planet, as we know it, will be gone. What kind of new world will there be for the righteous was unclear to Peter. But the heavens and elements (*stoixeia*) of the present will be no more. Bigg thought that Peter was using the word for elements to describe purely physical composition as the ancients did: the elements of earth, air, water, and fire. [16]

Whatever Peter meant, a whole new prism of thought accompanied his concept of the *parousia*. The present surroundings will be gone, and a new habitat will follow. Peter offered this addition to our knowledge of the *parousia* as well as the assurance that time meant very little to God. The moral persuasion that God cares for those lost souls not yet reached lent credence to Peter's arguments. Peter was confirming the other New Testament writers in wishing fervently that the gospel message could reach the vast number of unbelievers. Did Peter's arguments ease the intense concerns of his readers? The answer will never be known from his writings, but doubters probably remained. Often the heart wins over the mind. The hope of a quick return had been misunderstood. Even the New Testament writers had to curb their enthusiasm for an immediate *parousia*. Expectations of *parousia* were great throughout the church, especially during times of stress and persecution. Further comments on this coming of Christ were discussed by Jude in his letter.

Jude's letter is of similar content as the second letter of Peter. Jude was the brother of James, the leader of the Jerusalem church, and relied heavily upon Jewish writings and traditions. His short letter was full of warnings and predictions of judgment. Jude referred to the *parousia* as a coming and quotes from the writings of Enoch for support. The writings of Enoch were given credence in the tradition of the Jewish fellowship during this period of time. Judgment (*krisis*) and conviction were key words in his letter as verse 15 confirms.

Jude reminded his readers that they were living in the last period of time (*eskato chrono*). These words were similar to those of Paul to Timothy, to Peter's words in the second letter, and to the first letter of John (the last hour, *eskate hora*). In this way, Jude was explaining his firm belief that not much time is left for repentance. Some have already been judged; these beings included fallen angels, Sodom and Gomorrah, Cain, Balaam, Korah, and even Satan. Jude admonished his readers to "keep yourselves in the love of God, looking for the mercy of our Lord Jesus Christ unto eternal life" (Jude 1:21). The *parousia* was near and also the time of judgment. The Lord will come with countless (myriads) of His holy ones. The intensity of the *parousia* can be felt throughout the letter, written about the time of Second Peter. Bigg rendered his explanation of the mood of the epistle, "The style and tone of the Epistle set before us a stern and unbending nature." Jude had found the *parousia* to be certain, and Christians must be prepared for its arrival. [17]

In the writings of John, we can see *parousia* in both his letters and the Book of Revelation. In his first letter, John used the word *parousia* (coming) and the word *phaneroo* (appearance). In First John 2:28 he wrote, "And now, little children, abide in Him, that when He appears, we may have confidence and not be ashamed before Him at His coming." This verse is the only verse where John uses the word *parousia*, but he uses *phaneroo* several times in the letter. The word *phaneroo* can mean to make visible, make manifest, make clear. Perhaps the most familiar of the many uses of this word is in John 1:2; "And the life was manifested." In this passage, John was referring to the appearance of Christ into the world. In First John 2:28, John was referring to another appearance. This appearance was referring to Christ's coming or *parousia*. In his commentary Westcott acknowledged that while *parousia* did not occur elsewhere in this letter, "it is used as in exactly the same sense as it bears in all the other groups of apostolic writings." [18]

John was visualizing the present world being brought to a close.

Westcott stated, "The world exists indeed, but more as a semblance than a reality. It is overcome finally and forever. It is on the point of vanishing. This outward consummation is in God's hands. And over against the world there is the church, the organized Christian society, the depositing of the Truth and the witness for the Truth." [19]

John also used the term Antichrist as a sign for the end of time: "And even as you heard that Antichrist is coming, also now antichrists may have come to be, whence we know that it is the final hour" (First John 2:18). Lenski commented, "None of the apostles knew the day or the hour of the *parousia*. John saw the first group of antichrists." [20] As history continued, Christians continued to see Antichrist in various forms. Lenski summarized, "In the following ages new kinds of antichristian leaders arose. Church history describes them and the extent and the duration of the various movements." [21]

Thus for John, Christ will be made manifest or clear for all generations of humanity at the *parousia*. In the meantime, antichristian leaders will continue to make their appearance until the final appearance of Christ to the world.

The last book of apocalyptic writings occurred in Revelation. This letter is full of both fascination and enigma. The word *parousia* is not found in Revelation; however, the word *apokalalypsis*, or the revelation or uncovering, can describe the book.

Lenski wrote, "Revelation is a book of Promise and Judgment. The promise is intended for those who are sealed; the Judgment is intended for Satan and for those who are allied with him. While both Promise and Judgment attain their consummation at the last day, this climax is assured at every preceding step. The final outcome is inevitable. God's apocalypse had to do this unveiling in figurative, symbolic language. This is on our account. It is the adequate means for the effect to be attained, a true and decisive realization of the realities which confront us. We are the stake in the battle; our eyes must be opened timely to see. The figures and the symbols exceed all literal language in attaining this divine effect. We minimize and even lose this effect when we seek to translate this symbolic language into literal equivalents and then grow discouraged when we find it cannot be done." [22]

In Revelation, the final triumph of Christ occurred in chapters 21 and 22. All the battles have been fought, whether literal or symbolic in the reader's viewpoint. The last chapter of the letter has recorded the victory of Christ over Satan. This assumption included the saints with God in triumph. These saints have undergone persecution, even martyrdom. Christ was pictured as the ultimate conqueror. As

Hendriksen wrote in his commentary, "He conquers death, Hades, the dragon, the beast, the false prophet, the men who worship the beast, etc. He is victorious; hence, so are we! Even when we seem to be hopelessly defeated." [23]

Many points of view have continued to abound in regards to the book of Revelation and its relationship to Christians today. Many will agree with Hendriksen that the book was "God's answer to the prayers and tears of severely persecuted Christians scattered about in the cities of Asia-Minor." However many must also agree with him "that the admonitions and consolations of this book were meant for the entire church throughout the centuries." [24]

In Revelation 20:11–15, in place of *parousia* or coming, the scene changed to the judgment. The resurrected were before the throne of God, and books were opened. If anyone was not found as having been written in the Book of Life, the same was thrown into the lake of fire. In Revelation 21: 1-8, the judgment was expanded to include the new heaven and the new earth. The new city of Jerusalem was described in magnificent terms. John gave us a vision of the *parousia* that no other writer gave, for he described the heavenly city, the new Jerusalem where the saints will live in eternity. John closed not only with the promise of the coming of Jesus, but the triumph of the saints.

Chapter Six

Summary

Parousia is found throughout the New Testament both as a word and as a concept. The word is associated with hope, judgment, finality, and watchfulness. The word is not to be used by Christians in an anxious, frenetic way. The tenor of thought and concept by the New Testament writers is patience, forbearance, even endurance. Predictions for the *parousia* are not definite even though a healthy expectation is present. At times, the writers implore Jesus to return.

It can be debated whether a similar wish for the *parousia* pervades modern society. Even more distressing is the twisting of hopeful expectation into a manic searching for hidden signs of an immediate return. These kinds of speculations have been played out in every generation with utter futility. The *parousia* is on God's celestial clock, which means simply that there are no earthly time constraints. Christ will come. This is the great hope and fear of all generations.

Selected Sources

The Bible, various translations.

Bigg, Charles. *The International Critical Commentary: St. Peter and Jude.* Edinburgh: T and T Clark, 1987.

Hendriksen, W. *More than Conquerors: An Interpretation of the Book of Revelation.* Grand Rapids: Baker Book House, 1998.

Lenski, R.C.H. *The Interpretation of the Epistle to the Hebrews and the Epistle of James.* Minneapolis: Augsburg Publishing House, 1966.

Lenski, R.C.H. *The Interpretation of I and II Epistles of Peter, and Three Epistles of John, and the Epistle of Jude.* Minneapolis: Augsburg Publishing House, 1966.

Lenski, R.C.H. *The Interpretation of St. John's Revelation.* Minneapolis: Augsburg Publishing House, 1961.

Lightfoot, J.B. *Notes on the Epistles of St. Paul.* Grand Rapids: Zondervan Publishing House, 1957.

McGarvey, J.W. *A Commentary on Matthew and Mark.* Delight, Arkansas: Gospel Light Publishing Company, 1875.

Selected Sources

Plummer, Alfred. *An Exegetical Commentary on the Gospel According to St. Matthew*. Grand Rapids: Wm. B. Eerdman's Publishing Company, 1956.

Rackham, R.B. *The Acts of the Apostles*. London: Methuen and Company, Ltd. 1957.

Robertson, Archibald, and Alfred Plummer. *The International Critical Commentary: I Corinthians*. Edinburgh: T and T Clark, 1961.

Walker, Rollin. "Thessalonica." *The International Standard Bible Encyclopedia*. Grand Rapids: Wm. B. Eerdman's Publishing House, 1960.

Westcott, B.F. *The Epistle to the Hebrews*. Grand Rapid: Wm.B. Eerdman's Publishing Company, 1892.

Westcott, B.F. *The Epistles of St. John*. Grand Rapids: Wm. B. Eerdman's Publishing Company, 1957.

End Notes

1. *An Exegetical Commentary on the Gospel of St. Matthew*, Alfred Plummer, 1956, Wm. B. Eerdmans Publishing Company

2. *A Commentary on Matthew and Mark*. J.W. McGarvey, 1875, Gospel Light Publishing Company

3. *An Exegetical Commentary on the Gospel of St. Matthew*, Alfred Plummer, 1956, Wm. B. Eerdmans Publishing Company

4. *The Acts of the Apostles*, R.B. Rackham, 1957, Methuen and Company Ltd.

5. Ibid

6. *The International Critical Commentary, I Corinthians*, Archibald Robertson and Alfred Plummer, 1961, T and T Clark

7. *Notes on the Epistles of St. Paul, J.B. Lightfoot*, 1957, Zondervan Publishing House

8. *The International Standard Bible Encyclopedia*, " Thessalonica" Rollin Walker, 1960, Wm.B. Eerdmans Publishing House

9. *The Epistle to the Hebrews*, B.F. Westcott, 1892, Wm. B. Publishing Company

10. Ibid

11. Ibid

12. *The Interpretation of the Epistle of Hebrews and the Epistle of James*, R.C.H. Lenski, 1966, Augsburg Publishing House

13. Ibid

End Notes

14. *The International Critical Commentary, St. Peter and Jude,* Charles Bigg, 1987, T and T Clark

15. Ibid

16. Ibid

17. Ibid

18. *The Epistles of St. John*, B.F. Westcott, 1957, Wm.B. Eerdmans Publishing Company

19. Ibid

20. *The Interpretation of the First and Second Epistles of Peter, and Three Epistles of John, and the Epistle of Jude,* R.C.H. Lenski, 1966, Augsburg Publishing House

21. Ibid

22. *The Interpretation of St. John's Revelation*, R.C.H. Lenski, 1961, Augsburg Publishing House

23. *More Than Conquerors, An Interpretation of the Book of Revelation*, W. Hendriksen, 1998, Baker Book House

24. Ibid

Part Two: Description

Heavenly Words

Descriptions of Heaven in the New Testament

Chapter Seven
Foreshadows of Heaven

From the very beginning of scripture, the words for heaven or heavens were mentioned: "God created the heavens and the earth" (Genesis 1). The Hebrew word *shamayem* corresponded to the Greek word *ouranoi*. Both words can refer to the physical concept of heavenly places such as planets and stars, or to celestial realms–the abode of God and His angels. In Old Testament times, the heavens were presented as evidences of God's power and majesty. The Wisdom books are full of references to the heavenly glory of God as demonstrated by His creative strength. Examples follow:

Psalms 8:34 is one such example: "When I consider the heavens, the work of thy fingers, the moon and the stars, which thou hast ordained; What is man that thou dost take thought of him? And the son of man, that thou dost care for him?"

In Job 38:31 Job was asked, "Can you bind the chains of the Pleiades, or loose the cords of Orion? Can you lead forth a constellation in its season, and guide the Bear with her satellites? Do you know the ordinances of the heavens or fix their rule over the earth?"

"For all the gods of the peoples are idols, but the Lord made the heavens" (Psalms 96:5).

"The Lord has established His throne in the heavens, and His sovereignty rules over all" (Psalms 103:19).

The prophets continued with an examination of the heavens. Isaiah was perhaps the best known of the celestial prophets, for in Isaiah 66:1 he wrote, "Thus says the Lord, 'Heaven is My throne and the earth is my footstool. Where then is a house you could build for Me? And where is a place that I may rest?'"

Other passages from the Old Testament reflected an interest in the heavens. The author of Genesis recorded the dream of Jacob in Genesis 28: "And he had a dream, and behold a ladder was set on the earth with its top reaching the heavens: and behold, the angels of God were ascending and descending on it." The author of Second

Kings recounted Elijah's ascent to heaven in II Kings 2:11; "Then it came about as they were going along and talking that behold, there appeared a chariot of fire and horses of fire which separated the two of them. And Elijah went up by a whirlwind to heaven."

In this section of the book, our interest will be focused on New Testament passages that refer to heaven and its meaning for the believers of all periods of time

Chapter Eight
The Kingdom of Heaven

The term for kingdom of heaven (*basileia ton ouranon*) was used extensively by the New Testament writers, particularly by Matthew in his gospel. Heaven was used by Matthew, not particularly relating to God's abode, but rather to the domain of the followers of Christ. In Matthew 4:23 when Jesus began His ministry, Matthew described the advent of this ministry with these words, "And Jesus went about in all Galilee, teaching in their synagogues, and preaching the gospel of the kingdom." The parables in Matthew 13:11, which formed so large and prominent a portion of His teaching, were described collectively as "the mysteries of the kingdom of heaven." Many of these parables commenced with the phrase "the kingdom of heaven is like...." In the words of one commentator, "Jesus is, however, aware of a region in the universe where the will of God is at present being perfectly and universally done. It explains the social side of Christianity. A kingdom implies multitude and variety, and though religion begins with the individual, it must aim at brotherhood, organization, and expansion. It explains loyalty. However much kings and kingdoms may fail to touch the imagination in an age of the world when many countries have become or are becoming republican, the strength to conquer and endure will always have to be derived from contact with personalities. It keeps alive the truth, suggested by Jesus in the Lord's Prayer, that the doing of the will of God on earth is the one thing needful. This is the true end of all authority in both church and state, and behind all efforts thus directed there is at work the potency of heaven. It reminds all generations of men that their true home and destiny is heaven." [1]

Many attempts have been made to create a literal kingdom of heaven on earth. These utopian attempts have always failed. Jesus was not talking about any earthly kingdom. His references to the kingdom of heaven were all in preparation for a future existence. In Matthew 13, Jesus delivered a succession of parables which compared the kingdom to the process of sowing seed, the growth of the seed, the treasure found in a field, the merchant seeking beautiful pearls, and the fisherman netting a catch. These similes were progressive in nature as humans chose certain valuable objects or planted valuable seed. Those who made incorrect choices were caught up and cast out just as bad fish were thrown away.

In Matthew 18, Jesus illustrated who will be the greatest in the kingdom of heaven: "And he called a child to Himself and stood in their midst and said, 'Truly I say to you, unless you are converted and become like children, you shall not enter the kingdom of heaven. Whoever then humbles himself as this child, he is the greatest in the kingdom of heaven.'" This spirit of gentleness of the kingdom was found not only in the references to children but with those in power. In the same chapter, Matthew recorded Jesus referring to a king and his servants. The king was kind to a servant. However, the servant was rude and cruel towards a fellow servant. Because of his cruel spirit, the king must reject and punish the first servant. In Matthew 20, the parable was about a generous land owner who rewarded all of his laborers equally. This equity was despised by other workers who had labored longer, and who believed they were owed more. The landowner was resolute in his generosity towards all of the faithful servants. Such was the kingdom of heaven.

In Matthew's gospel, Jesus warned that the kingdom of heaven will come when least expected. The bridal attendants in Matthew 25 were not prepared for the arrival of the bridal party. Thus, they were excluded from the bridal feast. From this parable Jesus taught that the life of the kingdom did not create power on earth, but for heaven. The preparation needed for the heavenly kingdom was generosity and patience. Those who will be accepted in the kingdom of heaven will be of such nature. As one writer concluded about the kingdom of heaven, "In not a few of Our Lord's own sayings, as has been remarked, our phrase is obviously only a name for heaven, and while His aim was that the kingdom ought to be established on earth, He always promised to those aiding in its establishment in this world that their efforts would be rewarded in the world to come. The constant recognition of a spiritual and eternal world is one of the unfailing marks of genuine Christianity." [2]

Chapter Nine

The Heavenly House of God

In John 14:1–3 Jesus said to His disciples, "Let not your heart be troubled, believe in God, believe also in Me. In My Father's house are many dwelling places; if it were not so, I would have told you; for I go to prepare a place for you. And if I go and prepare a place for you, I will come again, and receive you to Myself; that where I am, there you may be also." The term Father's house was similar to the expression house of God (*oikos theou*) and was the concept of heaven as a community of believers. While kingdom denoted power, albeit spiritual, not worldly, a house or home referred to an intimate concept of the heavenly realm. The concept of God's house was one of endless rooms or abodes. The old Christian hymn that spoke of mansions in glory may be closer to the description of John's gospel simply because God's house never ends.

In Jewish tradition the concept of a house could range from a temple or palace to a modest hut. The earliest lodgings of the Jews were caves, and individuals lived there, either by necessity or by choice. Lot, the nephew of Abraham, lived in a cave with his two daughters after fleeing the cataclysm of Sodom. This cave was not by choice but provided temporary refuge. Genesis 19:30 revealed that Lot had a genuine fear of the city of Zoar; perhaps he was thinking of another firestorm. Thus, he went to a cave in the mountains hoping for some solace.

On the other hand, Elijah, an outdoorsman, would have looked for a cave as a permanent place of security (I Kings 19:9). Elijah would have been familiar with caves wherever he traveled in Israel. His counterpart in the New Testament, John the Baptist, must have been very familiar with caves as homes. Even Jesus in all probability spent time in a caves as He often went to the wilderness to pray and meditate.

The author of Hebrews pictured caves in a lesser light including them with places "in deserts and mountains and caves and holes in the ground" where the saints of God wandered (Hebrews 11:38).

The scriptures also described caves as the final house on earth such as the burial place or tomb of Lazarus.

Whatever these primitive caves signified in the way of houses, most Jews thought of stone or mud and brick dwellings as a house (*oikos*). One could be more cheerful in such a dwelling whether it was a simple hut of one story or a more elaborate dwelling with apartments and attachments. As in modern times, the house or home had to have strong foundations. Hence there were many references to foundations and cornerstones in the New Testament. Peter quoted from Psalm 118 when talking about Jesus becoming the chief cornerstone of our faith. Part of the home's structure consisted of flooring, dirt in most houses, with stone slabs in the houses of the middle and upper classes. Every home had a door, and the Israelites placed great value on the door as a symbol of God's protection as during the Passover feast and also as a symbol of hospitality.

The roof of the house was also very important because of the utilitarian nature of its flat surface. It could be used as a place of prayer and as a meeting place. In Luke 5:19 the tiled roof (*keramos*) was mentioned in the story where a man was let down through the roof to see Jesus. Literally, the people had to tear up the roof top (*doma*) to expedite their plan. In addition, many homes also had apartments or chambers; Jesus must have been talking about these apartments when he used the word *mone* in John 14: "In My Father's house are many chambers." The translation *mansions* would be accurate for God's chambers, which must be like mansions to people on earth.

Of course, the description of heaven as a home conjured up more than brick and mortar. Jesus often described Himself on earth as without a permanent home while He ministered. However, in His days before the public ministry, He was privileged to live in a Godly home with His earthly parents. Joseph and Mary were His home, and here He learned the craft of a carpenter. While in the days of ministry, approximately three years, He did enjoy the home of Mary, Martha, and Lazarus. He also went to the homes of certified sinners such as Zacchaeus, a chief tax collector (Luke 19).

The idea of a heavenly home would stir up fond memories of hospitality and love for the disciples of Jesus just as the word home does today. Even today, souls who do not have a happy earthly home still wish for that ideal home where happiness abounds. In its broadest sense, Heaven will be a spiritual kingdom, a happy dwelling place with an unlimited amount of love for those who will enjoy its glory forever.

Chapter Ten

A Heavenly Paradise

The word paradise (*paradeisos*) was used only three times in the New Testament, and Jesus used it only once in Luke 23:43. The word was translated from the Hebrew as *pardes* and is probably Persian in origin. Nehemiah used the word in Nehemiah 2:8 when he requested a letter be sent to the "King's keeper of the forest." The word was transferred to Hebrew during this period although the Hebrews used a similar word for a place of vegetation, in this case a garden as in the "garden of Eden" in Genesis 2:15.

The word for paradise in the Old Testament suggested a tangible place where lush vegetation abounds. Ezekiel also used the word to describe a vision, and he must have been familiar with Persian terminology such as in the beauty of a beautiful, cultivated park.

As mentioned, Jesus used the word but once, and to a stranger, the thief on the cross. The British scholar Alfred Plummer commented, "By His use of the word, Jesus neither confesses nor corrects Jewish beliefs on the subject. He assures the penitent that He will do far more than remember him at some unknown time in the future: this very day He will have him in His company in a place of security and bliss."[3] G. F. Wright elaborated, "The consolation needed by the penitent thief suffering from thirst and agony and shame was such as was symbolized by the popular conception of paradise." Wright concluded that Jesus used other allusions to heaven that were similar to a garden but were in contrast to the misinterpreted sensuality of some Islamic concepts. The marriage supper described in Matthew 25 emphasized a physical, yet tasteful, preparation for the new kingdom. [4]

Paul used the word paradise when referring to a vision he experienced which he documented in Second Corinthians 12:1–4: "Boasting is necessary though it is not profitable, but I will go on to visions and revelations of the Lord. I know a man in Christ who fourteen years ago, whether in the body I do not know, or out of the body I do not know, God knows; such a man was caught, whether in the body or apart from the body I do not know, God knows, up into paradise, and had heard inexpressible words, which a man is not permitted to speak." In his studies of Second Corinthians, Plummer wrote that Paul "reluctantly, and only for a moment" lifted the veil which usually covered the details of the most sacred moments of his life and allowed the Corinthians to see enough. He could doubt his own identity with the recipient rather than doubt the revelation, and he speaks of the revelations as if they had been experienced by someone who, during those mysterious times, was one other than himself. As to the word paradise that Paul used, Plummer wrote, "The word tells us little about the nature of the unseen world. In the O. T. it is used either of the Garden of Eden or of a park or pleasure ground." Plummer concluded that we must leave open the question as to whether Paul regarded "paradise and the third heaven as identical, or as quite different, or as containing the other for there is no clue to the answer." [5]

Thus, in Second Corinthians Paul added little to our understanding of the word paradise other than the common view, and one that he must have held: that the concepts of paradise and heaven were very similar. Whether paradise can be literally interpreted as a level of heaven is certainly open to dispute. Jewish traditions included seven heavens, but seven was a number of perfection; the numbers three, seven, or twelve were often used symbolically for completeness.

In Revelation 2:7, the Apostle John returned to the idea of a paradise garden. He referenced the garden where the tree of life flourished, The Garden of Eden. Such pastoral references were quite prominent during the Renaissance. Writers McDannell and Lang mentioned the Renaissance picture of heaven as a beautiful garden populated by the saints of all ages. Using illustrations from Fra Angelico, Bosch, and Valla, these writers stated, "When Valla imagines the saints flying like birds and playing in mid air or diving into the sea like fish, he may exaggerate Renaissance dreams; yet he gives expression to a common sentiment. If Paradise is to be human, then it cannot be a place of inactivity and immobility. The Renaissance celebration of sensuous paradise had little time to flourish. It subsided as the Reformation put new facts onto the agenda of intellectual Europe. Only one idea survived: the idea of the heavenly reunion." [6]

This idea of paradise has not been prominent in Christian thought because a tangible concept of heaven seemed to detract from the spiritual nature of the afterlife. However, this word was used as one description of heaven, and the word did imply gifts and pleasures similar yet superior to the most desired on earth. Jacques Jomier commented that the Islamic concept of paradise has been taken out of context where "the promise of women of paradise (*houris*) have sometimes been developed to a degree of crudity which is difficult to take in popular literature. However, the climax of happiness will consist of knowing that one is accepted by God and is being happy with Him." [7]

We can summarize by saying that the sparse use of the word paradise in the scriptures did not necessarily obviate or diminish its importance. Although there was a paucity of comments about paradise in the New Testament, when the word paradise was used, the meaning was clear. Heaven must be thought as the most pleasant existence, with tangible pleasures far exceeding those on earth.

Chapter Eleven

Heavenly Citizenship

In Philippians the Apostle Paul was thinking a lot about heaven. Perhaps it was because of his circumstances. He was in prison and was concerned about many things, including his own mortality. The Philippian church had revived their interest in him. The messenger Epaphroditus had brought him "a fragrant aroma, an acceptable sacrifice, well pleasing to God" (Philippians 4:18). Paul had learned to be self sufficient in whatever circumstances that he found himself (Philipians 4:11). The Greek word that he used was *autarkes*, meaning resourceful and satisfied; in a philosophical sense the word meant to be independent. This word was also used in First Timothy 6:6 when

Paul wrote that "godliness actually is a means of great gain when accompanied by contentment or satisfaction."

Paul's contentment or satisfaction had limitations. At times he felt lonely, at other times joyous. Sometimes he longed deeply for heaven. In Philippians 1:21-24 he wrote, "For to me, to live is Christ, and to die is gain. But if I am to live on in the flesh, this will mean fruitful labor for me; and I do not know which to choose. But I am hard pressed from both directions, having the desire to depart and be with Christ, for that is very much better; yet to remain on in the flesh is more necessary for your sake." Throughout this book Paul was longing for heaven. The average lifespan of his day was around 50 years of age. His body was broken from all of the persecutions he had endured, which included even stoning. A spark of resilience was still within him, and he wanted to continue guiding fellow Christians. He had reached a point in his spiritual life where he could be self sufficient through Christ. He knew how to "get along with humble means" and "how to live in prosperity; in any and every circumstance I have learned the secret of being filled and going hungry, both of having abundance and suffering need" (Philippians 4:12).

Paul knew that heaven was the Christian's ultimate goal. In Philippians 3:14 he wrote, "I press on toward the goal for the prize of the upward call of God in Christ Jesus." In Philippians 3:20 he wrote,

"For our citizenship is in heaven, from which also we eagerly wait for a Saviour, the Lord Jesus Christ." The Greek word for citizenship was *politeuma*, or community of citizens. This word can also be translated as a colony of people.

Citizenship was much prized in the Roman Empire. In Acts 22:28, the Roman *Chiliarch*, who was in charge of Paul, said that he had acquired his citizenship at a great cost in money. Paul replied that he himself was actually born a citizen. In Acts 23:1, Paul spoke to the Sanhedrin and reminded them that he had lived and continued to live in "good citizenship before God." In Philippians 1:27 he urged his readers to "live as citizens" in a worthy manner in regards to the gospel of Christ.

Paul regarded citizenship to be the highest form of reward in the Roman Empire. Citizenship afforded him many opportunities including a chance to appeal his situation to Caesar. For him, citizenship in heaven was an even greater reward. Heaven would be a place where all the believers would share community. All would be treated with the same dignity and glory in the presence of Christ.

In his book *The Greeks*, H.D.F. Kitto explained the Greek concept of community or *polis*. It is "an active, formative thing, training the minds and characters of the citizens." Pericles, the great Greek statesman, thought of the *polis* as a way of life, and all citizens could participate in a common cultural life. [8] However, citizenship would have been an almost alien word to most people of the first century. Slave populations varied in the large cities, with Athens and Rome numbering in the hundreds of thousands. Paul, realizing that many of his fellow Christians were slaves, used the word *doulos* or slave to describe himself. In fact he began his letter to the Romans by describing himself as a slave of Jesus Christ (Romans 1:1). In Galatians during one of his most eloquent conclusions in regards to different classes of society, the apostle seemed to grasp the entire sweep of social reform and made clear that the earthly distinctions of class and gender were unknown to Christ "as there is neither Jew nor Greek, male nor female, for you are all one in Christ Jesus" (Galatians 3:28). In Philippians 1:1 he addressed himself and Timothy as "slaves of Christ Jesus to all the saints in Christ Jesus who are in Philippi, including the overseers and deacons."

James used the same slave description in his letter. He was a "slave of God and the Lord Jesus Christ" (James 1:1). Peter used similar language in Second Peter 1:1 when he began, "Simon Peter, a slave and apostle of Jesus Christ to those who have received a faith of the same kind as ours, by the righteousness of God and Savior, Jesus Christ." Jude also used the word *doulos* when he wrote, "Jude, a slave of Jesus

Christ, and brother of James to those who are the called, beloved in God the Father, and kept for Jesus Christ" (Jude 1).

Since citizenship on earth was only a remote hope for many Christians of Paul's time, the word *hetaeria* was often used. The word describes an organization such as a guild or society. Robert Wilken, in his book *The Christians as the Romans Saw Them*, mentioned that this word, whether used by Christians or not, was thought to be an apt description of Christianity. Wilken cited the Emperor Trajan as an example of one who thought of the Christians in this way. Trajan saw such societies or clubs as "social organizations, and the members met together regularly for food and drink, fun and relaxation, and support in times of trouble. As a consequence, they were a natural breeding ground for grumbling about the conduct of civic affairs and they often became involved in politics." [9] Such a word was used in the New Testament only by Matthew and was translated as companion, comrade, or friend. In the parable of the wedding feast, the king addressed the unprepared guest as a *hetairon*, a comrade or companion (Matthew 22:12). In Matthew 20:13, the landowner described the grumbling worker as *hetairos* or comrade. In conclusion, the word *hetairos* could not be used to mean best friend. But the word described a community that the Christians, in the eyes of the Romans, had to a great degree.

According to Wilken, the Romans saw the Christians as a community or society involved in both a *superstitio*, an illegal religion, and a political caucus. He noted that the plural term *hetaeria* was a transliteration into Latin of a Greek word originally rendered political club. As conclusive evidence, part of Pliny's letter to Trajan was quoted: "They also declared that the sum total of their guilt or error amounted to no more than this; they had met regularly before dawn on a fixed day to chant verses alternately among themselves in honor of Christ as if to a god, and also to bind themselves by oath; but they had in fact given up this practice since my edict, issued on your instructions, which banned all *hetaerias*."[10] From all this we can conclude that communities of believers existed in the first century and into the second century who desperately longed for citizenship, if not found on earth, then realized in heaven.

Chapter Twelve

A Heavenly Country

In Hebrews 11:16, the Hebrew writer concluded, "But as it is, they desire a better country, that is a heavenly one. Therefore God is not ashamed to be called their God; for He has prepared a city for them." The writer used two words: *patris* found in Hebrews 11:14 and *polis* in Hebrews 11:16. These words can be translated as homeland and city respectively. Jesus had used the word *patris* for his home town of Nazareth in John 4:44; "For Jesus Himself testified that a prophet has no honor in his own country." He also used this word to describe His other home town country of Capernaum as found in Luke 4:23. The word *polis* was used more frequently in the New

Testament, usually referring to a walled community as opposed to a simple village or *kome*.

In the Hebrew letter, the writer was describing the end of a journey for the faithful. Not only Abraham but all the Old Testament characters to some degree desired something better than this life. Abraham exercised his faith to a very high degree that B.F. Wescott described as "the faith of patient obedience. The faith of the patriarchs, represented by the Faith of Abraham, is presented under three different aspects: (1) As Abraham trusted God wholly, going forth he knew not whither (the faith of self-surrender); (2) as he waited on the scene of his hope looking for God's work (the faith of patience); (3) as he communicated his faith to Sarah, so that through them (one flesh) the innumerable offspring of faith were born (the faith of influence)." Wescott then commented, "The life of the patriarchs was a life of faith to the last, supported by trust in the invisible which they realized, resting on complete surrender, directed beyond earth. They showed that the true satisfaction of human powers, the city which answers to man's social instincts, must be heavenly." [11]

In reading Hebrews 11, one finds the metaphor of a journey quite often apparent. The examples of faith from Enoch through the period of the Judges demonstrated a way beset by trials, mistakes, misfortunes, and ineptitude. The characters of faith often fell far short of exemplary models of purity. Who can honestly hold up Jepthah or Samson as paragons of virtue? Yet, all of the characters of Hebrews 11 had a spark of faith that allowed them to see beyond the here and now to the heavenly country.

Many people have read Bunyan's work, *Pilgrims Progress*. This allegory, whose chief character was Christian, was written by an unremarkable Puritan by the name of John Bunyan. He lived his life as an uneducated tradesman, but his book was the most popular religious book of its day other than *The King James Bible*. He chose to write his book in an allegorical style, which was popular in his day, and chronicle the journey of Christian, the main character, through the various trials of the Christian life. In the journal *British Heritage*, of September 2006, Bruce Heydt wrote, "To the colonists, many of them Puritans themselves, America was not just the New World, but a better one, the embodiment of the promised New Jerusalem, the goal of Christian's quest." [12]

In later times, the metaphor of a journey was not lost on Americans of the nineteenth century. The journey of Lewis and Clark from Missouri to the Pacific Ocean in 1804–1806 was a phenomenal event. The brilliant American President Thomas Jefferson (ever the inquisitive scientist) wanted a full and documented exploration of the area acquired through the Louisiana Purchase of 1803. Dayton

Duncan and Ken Burns introduced their book *Lewis and Clark, the Journey of the Corps of Discovery* with the description, "One afternoon in the spring of 1804, in a heavy loaded keelboat and two oversized canoes, nearly four dozen men crossed the Mississippi River and started up the Missouri, struggling against its thick muddy current. They were on the most important expedition in American history– the United States' first official exploration into unknown spaces, and a glimpse into their young nation's future. They would be the first United States citizens to experience the Great Plains: the immensity of the skies, the rich splendor of its wildlife, the harsh rigors of its winters. They would be the first American citizens to see the daunting peaks of the Rocky Mountains, the first to struggle over them, the first to cross the Continental Divide to where the rivers flow west. And–after encountering cold, hunger, danger, and wonders beyond belief–they would become the first of their nation to reach the Pacific Ocean by land. It would be the greatest adventure of their lives." [13]

The Lewis and Clark expedition in many ways has paralleled the lives of faithful Christians. In their expedition, the explorers were met with many hardships, and they were given up for lost. Dangers were abundant, but the expedition lost only one explorer, and his loss was to fatal disease. The company of explorers was diverse with Sacagawea, a Shoshone Indian woman, as a guide along with her

French trader husband, Charbonneau. In addition, York, the African American slave of Clark, became a full voting partner on the journey. The expedition party befriended the Native Americans on many occasions. The whole journey was a remarkable combination of faith and providence.

For the Christian, Hebrews 11 will give hope that the patient faith of the believer will reap dividends. The journey will be troubled at times. The Promised Land will seem unreachable. However, as George Rogers Clark exclaimed when he saw the ocean for the first time, "O, the joy."[14] The Christian will experience even greater joy when the heavenly country is seen.

Chapter Thirteen

The Shaking of the Heavens

Geerhardus Vos wrote in an article on eschatology, "The scene of the consummate state is the new heaven and the new earth, which are called into being by the eschatological *palingenesis* (regeneration)." [15] In Hebrews 12:26–29, the writer proclaimed, "See to it that you do not refuse Him who is speaking. For if these did not escape when they refused him who warned them on earth, much less shall we escape who turn away from Him who warns form heaven. And this expression, yet once more, denotes the removing of those things which can be shaken, as of created things, in order that those things which cannot be shaken may remain. Therefore, since we receive a kingdom which cannot be shaken, let us show gratitude, by which we may offer to God an acceptable service with reverence and awe; for our God is a consuming fire." Although not used in this passage in Hebrews, the word for renewal or regeneration (*palingenesia*) was used in Titus to describe a rebirth created by Jesus Christ for the Christian. Matthew used the same word in Matthew 19:28 to describe an eschatological setting, the regeneration of humanity at the end of time.

When one talks about eschatology or the doctrine of last events, the question will arise as to the fate of this present world. Vos believed that, although destruction by fire will come as described in Second Peter 3:6–7, "an annihilation of the substance of the present world is not taught. The central abode of the redeemed will be in heaven, although the renewed earth will remain accessible to them and a part of the inheritance." [16]

Peter described a destruction of the elements or *stoixeia* in Second Peter 3. This word could mean the basic materials of the natural world or the demons of nature (Colossians 2:8). David Winter, in his excellent book *Hereafter*, described this new place called heaven: "The important thing is that heaven is where God is (the dwelling of God is with men) and in this new heaven God has drawn His people into a community in which He is going to dwell. We are not defending some dark or hidden corner of the universe where we imagine heaven may be located. Heaven is not in a corner anywhere and it will never be located by even the most powerful radio telescopes. It is simply not in this world. It is not in their dimension: up, down, or sideways." [17] Whether we agree with Winter or accept Vos's interpretation, the scriptures are plain that this present earth and heavenly surroundings will be changed and purified. The word regeneration means a new birth. The evil that surrounds the Christian will be destroyed. The new world will be a sanctified world. A shaking of the present world will happen at the *parousia*, the second coming, when Christ will return in triumph. This change will be completed with the shaking of the Heavens.

Chapter Fourteen

The Heavenly Body

In Acts 17, the Apostle Paul preached one of his most famous sermons. Passages from this sermon have often been quoted in church gatherings. What has been often forgotten is that this sermon was not well received by most of the Athenians. In Acts 17:32 we read, "Now when they heard of the resurrection of the dead, some began to sneer, but others said, 'We shall hear you again concerning this.'"

This would not be the last time that Paul would have to explain the heavenly or resurrected body. The Greeks and the Romans of Paul's day had a shadowy concept of the hereafter. Robert Garland wrote in his book, *The Greek Way of Death*, "While largely spared the horrors of a Christian Hell, the dying lacked as well the consolation of a better lot in the hereafter. It is therefore difficult to imagine that they can have contemplated their arrival in the world below with a more positive attitude of mind than that of restrained foreboding. To this limited extent, therefore, Hades, the place of darkness, was viewed by the Greeks as man's reward for Original Sin." [18] He concluded, "The ordinary Greek dead were more to be pitied than to be feared. Sterile, deadlocked in time, conscious of loss, out of touch with the world above, lacking the sinews and strength of the living, yet preserving everlastingly their wounds, their rancour, their hatred–these are the ghosts of worn out mortals as Homer represents them. To what extent succeeding centuries modified this picture can only be guessed at though Homer's authority was such that it is unlikely to have been completely supplanted." [19]

The Greeks had a strong doubt in regards to a bodily survival in the Hadean world. Paul stunned his Athenian audience with the hope of such a bodily resurrection. *The Expositor's Greek Testament* states, "The idea of retribution beyond the grave would have been equally alien to the Stoic as to the Epicurean, and both Stoic and Epicurean alike would have ridiculed the idea of a resurrection of the body." [20] Other Greeks in New Testament times were less skeptical but quite uncertain as to what Paul meant by resurrection and what form the body would take in the hereafter.

In his most lengthy discourse on the resurrection, Paul answered at length this involved question asked by the Corinthian congregation. In the latter verses of the chapter 15 he wrote, "All flesh is not the same flesh, but there is one flesh of men, and another flesh of beasts, and another flesh of birds, and another of fish. There are also heavenly bodies and earthly bodies, but the glory of the heavenly is one, and the glory of the earthly is another. There is one glory of the sun, and another of the moon, and another glory of the stars; for stars differ from stars in glory. So also is the resurrection of the dead. It is sown a perishable body, it is raised an imperishable body; it is sown in dishonor, it is raised in glory; it is sown in weakness, it is raised in power; it is sown a natural body, it is raised a spiritual body. So also it is written, the first man, Adam, became a living soul. The last Adam became a life giving spirit. However, the spiritual is not the first, but the natural; then the spiritual. The first man is from the earth, earthly; the second man is from heaven. As is the earthly, so also are those who are earthly; and as is the heavenly, so also are those who are heavenly. And just as we have borne the image of the earthly, we shall also bear the image of the heavenly. Now I say this, brethren, that flesh and blood cannot inherit the kingdom of God; nor does the perishable inherit the imperishable" (I Corinthians 15:39-59).

In verse 47 of this chapter, Paul made the distinction between the *ges xoikos anthropos* and the *anthropos ex ouranou*. In every case in the New Testament, the word *ges* was used to speak of earth or land. This land would be soil subject to cultivation. In the parable of the sower in Matthew 13, Jesus referred to the rocky places where there was not much found ground or soil (*ges*). The word *xoikos* was only used in First Corinthians 15 and can be translated as made of dust. Paul emphasized the person (*anthropos*) of the dusty soil opposite the person of the heavenly reality. Such a great contrast had many implications for Paul, not only physically but spiritually. The heavenly person will no longer be subject to physical maladies, but will be the glorious image of holiness and reconciliation.

In verse 40 Paul used the terms *somata epurania* and *somata epigeia*, or bodies of the heaven and bodies of the earth. Plummer observed, "There is a wide difference between terrestrial and celestial bodies; and there is a further difference between one celestial body and another. The God who made the myriads of differences in one and the same universe can be credited with inexhaustible power. It is monstrous to suppose that He cannot fit a body to spirit. Therefore we must not place any limit to God's power with regard either to the difference between our present and our future body, or to relations between them. He has found a fit body for fish, fowl, cattle and mortal man; why not immortal man? Experience teaches that God finds a suitable body for every type of earthly life and every type of heavenly life." [21] The proper body for heaven has been designed by God for each person who is His child. The question remains as to whether we can have any clue as to what that body will resemble.

David Winter, in his previously mentioned book *Hereafter*, devoted one of his chapters to the heavenly body. For his prime example he recalled the resurrected body of Jesus Christ. Winter noted that the resurrected appearance of Christ changed in a physical sense. Mary of Magdala thought Him to be the gardener. Recognition by His fellow travelers to Emmaus did not occur until he disappeared from their presence. At the Sea of Galilee, His disciples did not immediately recognize Him. Other physical conditions changed. Before the resurrection He got tired, thirsty, and hungry. He suffered and bled before the resurrection. After the ressurrection He traveled distances with no hindrances and was not confined by space or time. Winter affirmed, "It was undoubtedly a real body. Hundreds of people could not have been so mistaken, especially when Jesus offered clear evidence of it. But it was not an earthbound body." [22]

The early Christians had questions about the heavenly body, but they were certain of future existence beyond this life. Wayne Meeks, in *The First Urban Christians*, described the expectations of Paul's disciples: "The Pauline world view is eschatological. The Christians believe that the coming of Jesus, his crucifixion and resurrection, have already set in motion a shift in the order of the world. They expect very soon an end of the present age, the return of Jesus, and the final judgment of both human and cosmic powers." [23] Therefore, questions about the body's continued existence were part and parcel of New Testament thought.

Paul gave his analysis on the basis of questions from two Greek cities with Christian assemblies, Corinth and Thessalonika. Did the early Christians misinterpret his teachings? Probably not, but Paul found that additional explanation was needed. Paul's answers about the heavenly body answered basic questions. As Winter clearly concluded, we are severely limited in this present life by time, space, and physical maladies. Winter saw in the resurrected body that the personality of each person continued to exist but in a much greater glory with a body no longer subject to the confinements of earth. He wrote, "So the body we are to have after death (the resurrection body) is a development, a refinement of our present one, which disintegrates at death. There is a relationship between them, but the spiritual body is infinitely higher and in every respect superior. The personality–the message–remains, but the transmitter is a much better one." [24]

Such a transformation became an integral part of the heavenly words found in the New Testament.

Chapter Fifteen

Heavenly Visions

Visions have been a vital part of God's revelation to humanity. In the Bible, however, there are only a few visions alluding to heaven. The first vision is found in Genesis 28:10–22. There we find Jacob spending the night at the city of Bethel, and while asleep, he dreams of a stairway to heaven. This vision was replete with heavenly creatures, most likely kinds of angels. A promise is made to Jacob by God that He will give him and his descendants the land of Canaan. John Willis, in his commentary on Genesis, described the ladder which Jacob saw as "more like a solid stairway or a slanting pavement. The ziggurat at Ur in Mesopotamia has a flight of stairs leading up to its top, where it was thought that there was an opening connecting heaven and earth. In light of his experience, Jacob thought of this place as the gate of heaven." [25] John Skinner in his commentary on Genesis thought figuratively of the gates of heaven being guarded by angels when he stated, "Its permanent religious significance is expressed with profound insight and truth in John 1:51."[26] In later Hebrew history, King David, although not experiencing what we would call a vision, found solace after the death of his child with the hope that he would go to him at the end of this life (II Samuel 12).

While visions in the Old Testament were not specifically relating to the heavenly realms as plainly as references in the New Testament, heavenly images began to appear especially in regards to a Promised Land. The New Testament indicated that the Patriarchs might have seen much farther than this life. The writer of Hebrews in chapter 11 spoke to the heavenly promises that these ancient ones experienced. In Hebrews 11:13–16, such promises were addressed: "All these died in faith, without receiving the promises, but having seen them and having welcomed them from a distance, and having confessed that they were strangers and exiles on the earth; for those who say such things make it clear that they are seeking a country of their own. And if they had been thinking of that country from which they went out, they would have had opportunity to return. But as it is, they desire a better country that is a heavenly one. Therefore

God is not ashamed to be called their God: for He has prepared a city for them."

The New Testament mentioned at least three distinct visions which are recorded in some detail. In Acts 7:55–56, we read of Stephen's martyrdom and accompanying vision: "But being full of the Holy Spirit, he gazed intently into heaven and saw the glory of God, and Jesus standing at the right hand of God, and he said Behold, I see the heavens opened up and the Son of Man standing at the right hand of God." In verse 59, at the point of death, Stephen cried out, "Lord Jesus, receive my spirit!" R. B. Rackham made note in his commentary of the significance of this heavenly vision when he wrote, "It is the first appearance of Jesus in his divine glory. At the transfiguration he had appeared in glory to Peter, James, and John, but on earth: now Stephen sees him in heaven." Rackham was quick to observe that such a heavenly vision was granted only to Stephen, Paul, and John and "is the proof of the apostolic testimony to his exaltation and of Stephen's own teaching." [27] This heavenly vision was very important in that Christ's messages of a future life and His own exaltation were firmly established for the fledgling church.

The second vision that has heavenly overtones is found in Paul's writings to the Corinthians. This vision was alluded to in an earlier discussion of the word paradise. In Second Corinthians 12, Paul wrote about his own experience with visions and revelations. He reluctantly revealed his own visions to buttress his credibility among the Corinthians. Plummer commented that Paul is "quite clear about what he knows and what he does not know. He knows that he was caught up even to the third heaven; about that there is no possibility of delusion. He was conscious of the transfer, and he vividly remembers that for a time he was in heaven. But he is not sure of the relation in which his spirit was to his body during the experience; about that his memory tells him nothing." [28] As mentioned previously, Jewish tradition enumerated several heavens, even up to seven. Paul experienced a vision which enveloped at least three and was persuaded that the experience was too sacred to put into words (*arretos*). The expression *arretos* was used only in this passage in the New Testament (Second Corinthians 12:4). This word conveyed a sacred meaning which strengthened Paul's credibility to the Corinthians. Paul used the word paradise (*paradeisos*) to describe the third heaven as Jesus used this same word to describe heaven to the thief on the cross. The overall concept was one of tangible beauty and grandeur.

The final heavenly vision in the New Testament was described by the Apostle John in the Book of Revelation. Without any question, John's revelations of heaven in chapters 21 and 22 were the most complete of the visions. One can argue that the whole of this book is a vision. The word revelation literally meant an unveiling of the hidden (*apokalupsis*). John's vision at the end of the book was that of a new (*kainos*) heaven and earth. The word new (*kainos*) can be translated as recently made or unused. Jesus used the word when he described disciples of the kingdom of heaven as like householders "who bring forth out of his treasure things new (*kainos*) and old" (Matthew 13:52). Lenski, in his commentary of this book, interpreted the newness of our heavenly personalities as similar to our own, "We shall be the same persons and have the same body and the same soul that we now have, but these made entirely new. Our newness begins with regeneration." [29]

Thus Revelation 21 and 22 portrayed the regenerated heaven and earth as Jesus had promised in Matthew 19:28; "And Jesus said to them, Truly I say to you, that you who have followed me, in the regeneration when the Son of Man will sit on His glorious throne, you shall also sit upon twelve thrones, judging the twelve tribes of Israel." In his vision, John gave visual panoramas of the new heaven: "God will be among His people…our tears will be wiped away; there will be no mourning or crying; there will be no pain; there will be the spiritual Jerusalem, perfect in size and magnificently appointed with precious metal and jewels"(Revelation 21:3–4, 10–11).

John was able to radiate in the glory of God and in the brilliance of the lamp of the Lamb. The crystal river reflected the beauty of the gardens in the heavenly city. Thus, all of John's visions were reminiscent of the Eastern paradise mentioned by both Jesus and Paul and discussed earlier at some length. John's lengthy vision portrayed the most exquisite and expansive imagery of the ancient world. His vision completed the trilogy of visions begun by Stephen and followed by Paul. In all three of these visions, the portrait was one of peace with God and the Son of God. For Stephen, his heavenly vision was a release from the sufferings of martyrdom. For the Apostle Paul, his heavenly vision validated his work on earth and gave added credence to his message. For John, his heavenly vision offered comfort to the persecuted of all ages, including his own banishment, with hope eternal in the New Jerusalem.

Chapter Sixteen

The Church Enrolled in Heaven

Ecclesia (or *ekklesia*) and *koinonia* are Greek words which have special meaning in the New Testament. These words did not originally have theological meaning but more mundane identification. From the time of the Greek historian Thucydides, *ekklesia* meant an assembly of people who might be meeting at a public place or council for the purpose of deliberating. *Koinonia*, from the earliest of Greek history, meant a fellowship, a community, or an association. Both words were somewhat similar in meaning, although *koinonia* took on a much more personal connotation in the New Testament. *Koine* became the community language of not only the Greeks, but the whole New Testament world.

Ekklesia reached its highest meaning in Hebrews 12:23 when the writer predicted that his listeners were on their way to "the general assembly and church of the first-born who are enrolled in heaven, and to God, the Judge of all, and to the spirits of righteous men made perfect." The heavenly register or list is taken from the earthly list of the heavenbound assembly or *ekklesia*. Previously the church had been used in the sense of an assembly of Christians gathered for worship. Paul used the word *ekklesia* to describe the assembly at Corinth (I Corinthians 14:19). In Philippians 4:15, Paul expanded the usage to include assemblies in one region such as Macedonia: "After I departed from Macedonia, no church shared with me in the matter of giving and receiving but you alone."

However, the writer of Hebrews elevated this assembled community to the realms of heaven. Other words, *patria* or *oikos*, were often thought of as synonymous with community. *Patria* in the New Testament is used in the expanded sense of the community of nations (Acts 3:25). The words *o oikos tou Theou*, the family or household of God, also refer to the church. In I Timothy 3:15, Paul wrote, "But in case I am delayed, I write so that you may know how one ought to conduct himself in the household of God, which is the church (*ekklesia*) of the living God, the pillar and support of the truth." Peter wrote in similar fashion, "For it is time for judgment to begin with the household of God; and if it begins with us first, what will the outcome be for those who do not obey the gospel of God" (I Peter 4:17). In this sense, the church was a great household, and the fellowship was not limited to ancestral or ethnic tradition but included believers from all nations.

Thus, the church is also a heavenly family. When Jesus promised the thief that He would see him in paradise, He had no earthly relationship to the thief. Yet, the thief was to be part of the family of God. In Hebrews 3:2, this family was extended to those who were faithful in God's house: "Now Moses was faithful in all His house as a servant, for a testimony of those things which were to be spoken later" (Hebrews 3:5). In Hebrews 11, the list of the faithful of the Old Testament is given and includes those who were not of Jewish origin such as Rahab and Ruth.

This idea of church as an assembled community was an eternal concept beginning with God's eternal purpose from the days of the Old Testament. In the New Testament, as has been mentioned, an even more intimate word was often used regarding community. That word is *koinonia* which, as with *ekklesia*, had its origins in everyday usage. In Luke 5:10, James and John were described as partners in a business way: "And so also James and John, sons of Zebedee, who were partners [*koinonoi*] with Simon." When the word *koinonia* was used in the spiritual sense, it defined what the *ekklesia* or assembled church ought to be. In Philemon Paul wrote, "Paul, a prisoner of Christ Jesus, and Timothy our brother, to Philemon our beloved brother and fellow worker, and to Apphia our sister, and to Archippus our fellow soldier, and to the church [*ekklesia*] in your house; Grace to you and peace from God our Father and the Lord Jesus Christ. I thank my God always making mention of you in my prayers. Because I hear of your love, and of the faith which you have toward the Lord Jesus, and toward all the saints; and I pray that the fellowship [*koinonia*] of your faith may become effective through the knowledge of every good thing which is in you for Christ's sake" (Philemon 1–6).

In this passage, Paul identified a church by its fellowship among its members. Without this fellowship, this gathering or *ekklesia* would only be a gathering without concern for one another. In Hebrews, the church of the first born has such a fellowship in heaven. The tone was festive with the gathering (*paneguris*) being one of celebration similar to the Grecian athletic games. Westcott wrote, "The word *paneguris*, which was used especially in the great national assemblies and sacred games of the Greeks, occurs only here in the N.T. Men are described as a church, a congregation gathered for the enjoyment of special rights, even as the angels are assembled for a great festival."[30] The eternal gathering of the saints in fellowship will be an endless celebration beyond our imaginations.

Chapter Seventeen

The Heavenly Sabbath Rest

In Hebrews 4:8–11 the writer reminded his readers, "For if Joshua had given them rest, he would not have spoken of another day after that. There remains therefore a Sabbath rest for the people of God. For the one who has entered His rest has himself also rested from his works, as God did from His. Let us therefore be diligent to enter that rest, lest anyone fall through following the same example of disobedience." In these verses, the writer was referring to a future place of repose that transcends earthly turmoil. The word *katapausis* can be translated as a calming of the winds, a tranquil abode.

In a metaphorical sense, the passage in Hebrews 4:11 referred to that heavenly sphere of blessedness where God lives and which is promised to persevering believers in Christ after the toils of earthly life are over. In verse nine of the same chapter, the writer mentioned the *sabbatismos* or Sabbath rest. Wescott interpreted, "The Sabbath rest answers to the creation as its proper consummation. The word is only used here in the New Testament and must refer to the eternal Lord's Day." [31] The final rest completed the creation, fall, and redemption cycle.

The reference to Joshua's entrance into the Promised Land was a great parallel to the Christian's journey. The writer of Hebrews was describing a journey by faith to an unseen destination. This life was pictured as a shadow of things to come, a taste of things divine. In Hebrews 10:1 we read of the "shadow of the good things to come." This life also was a shadow of God's eternal resting place.

Rest as it is used in Hebrews referred to a different plane of existence. It did not refer to inactivity but rather to a life which was not limited or hindered by the vicissitudes of earthly life. Rest for the Israelites meant a permanent home which they lacked before. The Christian's rest was far superior as it does not mean the conquering of a new land, nor the need to constantly protect such a land. Rest meant a complete access to God's place and to the joys of His eternal presence.

When will the Christian enjoy this heavenly rest? Many passages in the New Testament predicted that the joy would be immediate. Jesus promised paradise to the thief without delay. Paul desired to be with the Lord immediately when he wrote to the Philippians. The poor man at the rich man's palace went immediately to the bosom of Abraham at his death. The realization of the eternal rest will become instantaneous at the end of this life according to the Hebrew letter. The Pauline concept of the resurrected body, however, will happen at the final day or Judgment Day. The eternal rest will begin at the end of life when the spirit of the Christian reaches the realms of God's abode. The Judgment Day will complete the uniting of spirit with the resurrected body.

Chapter Eighteen

Final Thoughts about Heaven

The primary purpose of this section of the book has been to examine certain words in the New Testament which describe heaven. This has been a study that neither exhausted all the references regarding heaven nor attempted to answer the myriad questions concerning that eternal abode. Early in the gospel of Matthew, John the Baptist preached that the kingdom of heaven was at hand (Matthew 3:2). The Christian today must accept this statement and go beyond it for Christ has come to this earth. Early in His ministry, Jesus was baptized and "behold the heavens were opened, and He saw the Spirit of God descending as a dove and coming upon Him, and behold, a voice out of the heavens, saying, 'This is My beloved Son, in whom I am well pleased'" (Matthew 3:16, 17). Among other things, this passage revealed a heavenly world, not the one we live in, as the ultimate validation of the Christian era.

Jesus instructed each person to pray in this way: "Our Father who art in heaven, hallowed be thy name. Thy kingdom come, Thy will be done, on earth as it is in heaven" (Matthew 6:9–10). Again, the reaching out to a different world, a world separate and apart from this earth was taught by Jesus. The kingdom has not reached completion, but communication between God and mankind can be possible through Jesus Christ. In the Gospel of Luke, the author mentioned the messengers of heaven when Gabriel brings the message of hope to Mary, the mother of Christ, in the first chapter. Later in Luke 2:13, the writer recorded, "And suddenly there appeared with the angel a multitude of the heavenly host praising God and saying, 'Glory to God in the highest and on earth peace among men with whom He is pleased.'" Luke then narrated that the angels left the earth for the realm of heaven. Thus, both angels and Jesus Christ went from the earthly realm to the heavenly realm.

In our present age the concept of heaven has been very little considered, even ignored. In a book previously referenced, *Heaven a History* by McDannell and Lang, the authors observed, "In spite of the current revival of religious interest in America and Europe, the details of heavenly existence remain a low priority." Christians who believe in heaven are divided. "They feel comfortable with a detailed afterlife in the style of either the modern heaven (continuation of family, work, progress) or the theocentric heaven (beatific vision, heavenly light, robed angels singing eternal praise)." These writers finally concluded, "Although fundamentalists would discard the suggestion that heaven no longer is an active part of their belief system, eternal life has become an unknown place or a state of vague identity. Conservative Christians confront rationalized religion with a heightened sense of faith, religious feeling and community, but they do not return to the rich heavenly images of previous generations. The drama of the future is decidedly this-worldly. Nor does real or alleged empirical evidence generally dispel skepticism. Accounts of near-death experiences relate glimpses of what lies beyond death, but present no long-term narratives."[32]

However, in this study of heavenly words, many heavenly images have been found in the New Testament. As an example, one interesting passage in Hebrews 12:1 has remained popular with those believing in heavenly contact with earthly saints. The writer stated, "Therefore, let us also, seeing we have so great a cloud of witnesses encompassing us, lay aside every encumbrance and the sin which so easily beset us, and with patience run the race that is set before us."

Westcott interpreted the verse in this manner: "These champions of old time occupy the place of spectators, but they are more than spectators. They are spectators who interpret to us the meaning of our struggle, and who bear testimony to the certainty of our success if we strive lawfully." [33] The interpretation could vary from actual knowledge of earthly conditions to an example of fulfilled faith that encourages each Christian. Certainly, the important lesson to be learned was that heavenly beings rejoice in the triumphs of Christians. We have been told that the angels rejoice when a sinner repents. Thus, the connection between heaven and earth has continued to be real and vital to those who are living on the earth.

Moreover, in totality, the conclusions of this review of heavenly scriptures are very optimistic in nature. Whether one leans to the theocentric or the modern interpretation of heaven, or both, it is clear from the writers of the New Testament that heaven is not a mere abstraction. Heaven is shown to be the eternal panoply of experiences that are indescribable to mortals. In one beautiful example of our future in heaven, Paul described the resurrected, spiritual, and heavenly body that exceeds anything mortals have known. In another example, the disciples experienced a glimpse of this spiritual body when viewing the resurrected Jesus. Recognition was part of their experience although Jesus was obviously different from how they had previously known Him. His body no longer fainted from thirst or hunger, nor could His body suffer from the pains of this life. Thus, the Christian was exhorted by Paul not to fear death, but to anticipate the glories of a heaven that will come. Paul was very certain when he concluded that death has lost its sting. In his writings, Paul was in complete agreement with Jesus who encouraged his disciples as well as all Christians with the words, "I have prepared a place for you, in My Father's house where there are many dwelling places" (John 14:2).

Selected Sources

Duncan, Dayton and Ken Burns. *Lewis and Clark, The Journal of the Corp of Discovery*. New York: Alfred A. Knopf, 1997.

Garland, Robert. *The Greek Way of Death*. Ithaca, New York: Cornell University Press, 1985.

Heydt, Bruce. *British Heritage*. Leesburg, Virginia: British Heritage Journal, 2006.

Jomier, Jacques. *How to Understand Islam*. New York: The Crossroads Publishing Company, 1989.

Kitto, H.D.F. *The Greek*. Hammondsworth, England: Penguin Books, 1957.

Knowling, R.J. *The Acts of the Apostles, The Expositors Greek Testament*. Grand Rapids, Michigan: Wm. B. Eerdmans Publishing Company, 1960.

Lenski, R.C.H. *St. John's Revelation*. Minneapolis, Minnesota: Augsburg Publishing House, 1961.

McDannel, Colleen and Bernhard Lang. *Heaven a History*. New Haven and London: Yale University Press, 1988.

Selected Sources

Meeks, Wayne. *The First Urban Christians.* New Haven and London: Yale University Press, 2003.

Plummer, Alfred. *A Critical and Exegetical Commentary on the Gospel According to Saint Luke.* Edinburgh: The International Critical Commentary, T and T Clark, 1960.

Plummer, Alfred and Archibald Robertson. *A Critical and Exegetical Commentary on the First Epistle of St. Paul to the Corinthians.* Edinburgh: The International Critical Commentary, T and T Clark, 1961.

Plummer, Alfred. *A Critical and Exegetical Commentary on the Second Epistle of St. Paul to to the Corinthians.* Edinburgh: The International Critical Commentary, T and T Clark, 1960.

Rackham, R.B. *The Acts of the Apostles.* London: Methuen and Company, 1957.

Skinner, John. *A Critical and Exegetical Commentary on Genesis.* Edinburgh: The International Critical Commentary, T and T Clark, 1980.

Selected Sources

Stalker, James T. "The Kingdom of God." *International Standard Bible Encyclopedia*. Grand Rapids, Michigan: Wm. B. Eerdmans Publishing Company, 1960.

Vos, Geerhardus. "Eschatology." *International Standard Bible Encyclopedia*. Grand Rapids, Michigan: Wm. B. Eerdmans Publishing Company, 1960.

Westcott, B.F. *The Epistle to the Hebrews*. Grand Rapids, Michigan: Wm.B. Eerdmans Publishing Company, 1970.

Wilken, Robert. *The Christians as the Romans Saw Them*. New Haven and London: Yale University Press, 2003.

Willis, John. *Genesis*. Austin, Texas: Sweet Publishing Company, 1979.

Winter, David. *Hereafter*. Wheaton, Illinois: Harold Shaw Publishing Company, 1973.

Wright, G.F. "Paradise." *International Standard Bible Encyclopedia*. Grand Rapids, Michigan: Wm. B. Eerdmans Publishing Company, 1960.

End Notes

1. *International Standard Bible Encyclopedia*, "The Kingdom of Heaven," James Stalker, 1960, Wm B. Eerdmans Publishing Company, Grand Rapids, Michigan

2. Ibid

3. *A Critical and Exegetical Commentary on the Gospel According to St. Luke*, Alfred Plummer, 1960, The International Critical Commentary, T and T Clark, Edinburgh

4. *International Standard Bible Encyclopedia*, "Paradise,: G.F. Wright, 1960, Wm. B. Eerdmans Publishing Company, Grand Rapids, Michigan

5. *A Critical and Exegetical Commentary on the Second Epistle of St. Paul to the Corinthians*, Alfred Plummer, 1960, The International Critical Commentary, T and T Clark, Edinburgh

6. *Heaven a History*, Coleen McDonnell, Bernhard Lang, 1988, Yale Unviversity Press, New Haven and London

7. *How to Understand Islam*, Jacques Jomier, 1989, The Crossword Publishing Company, New York

8. *The Greeks*, H.D.F. Kitto, 1957, Penguin Books, Hammondsworth, England

9. *The Christians as the Romans Saw Them*, Robert L. Wilken, 2003, Yale University Press, New Haven and London

10. Ibid

11. *The Epistle to the Hebrews*, B.F. Westcott, 1970, Wm. B. Eerdmans Publishing Company, Grand Rapids, Michigan

End Notes

12. *British Heritage*, Bruce Heydt, 2006, British Heritage Journal, Leesburg, Virginia

13. *Lewis and Clark*, The Journal of the Corp of Discovery, Dayton Duncan and Ken Burns, 1997, Alfred A. Knopf, New York

14. Ibid

15. *International Standard Bible Encyclopedia*, " Eschatology," Geerhardus Vos, 1960, Wm. B. Eerdmans Publishing Company, Grand Rapids, Michigan

16. Ibid.

17. *Hereafter*, David Winter, 1973, Harold Shaw Publishing Company, Wheaton Illinois

18. *The Greek Way of Death*, Robert Garland, 1985, Cornell University Press, Ithaca, New York

19. Ibid

20. *Expositors Greek Testament*, The Acts of the Apostles, 1960, R.J. Knowling, Wm. B. Eerdmans Publishing Company, Grand Rapids, Michigan

21. *A Critical and Exegetical Commentary on the First Epistle of St. Paul to the Corinthians*, Alfred Plummer and Archibald Robertson, 1961, The International Critical Commentary, T and T Clark, Edinburgh

22. *Hereafter, David Winter*, 1973, Harold Shaw Publishing Company, Wheaton, Illinois

End Notes

23. *The First Urban Christians*, Wayne Meeks, 2003, Yale University Press, New Haven and London

24. Hereafter, David Winter, 1973, Harold Shaw Publishing Company, Wheaton, Illinois

25. *Genesis*, John Willis, 1979, Sweet Publishing Company, Austin, Texas

26. *A Critical and Exegetical Commentary on Genesis, John Skinner*, 1980, The International Critical Commentary, T and T Clark, Edinburgh

27. *The Acts of the Apostles*, R.B. Rackham, 1957, Methuen and Company Ltd, London

28. *A Critical and Exegetical Commentary on the Second Epistle of St. Paul to the Corinthians*, Alfred Plummer, 1960, The International Critical Commentary, T and T Clark, Edinburgh

29. *St. John's Revelation, R.C.H. Lenski*, 1961, Augsburg Publishing House, Minneapolis, Minnesota

30. *The Epistle to the Hebrews*, B.F. Westcott, 1970, Wm. B. Eerdmans Publishing Company, Grand Rapids, Michigan

31. Ibid

32. *Heaven a History*, Colleen McDannell and Bernhard Lang, 1988, Yale University Press, New Haven and London

33. *The Epistle to the Hebrews*, B.F. Westcott, 1970, Wm.B. Eerdmans Publishing Company, Grand Rapids, Michigan

About the Author

James Byers is a graduate of David Lipscomb College, magna cum laude, and teaches an Asian Bible class at Harpeth Hills Church of Christ where he serves as a deacon. He has been a minister in congregations in Tennessee, Georgia, Flordia, and Hawaii. He had a career with the State of Tennessee as a teacher in Williamson County and with the Department of Human Services. He is married to the former Marie Potter, and they have one son, Tracy Byers, who is married to the former Evie Wade. James and Marie are also proud grandparents of three grandchildren. This is his second book with O'More Publishing.

...Also by James Byers

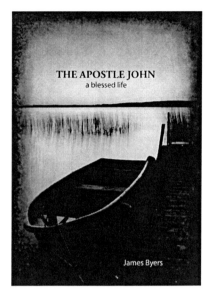

"John the Apostle was truly the Christian of the first century. His life spanned the rule of Augustus Caesar through Trajan; thus he lived through the reign of twelve emperors and died during the rule of the thirteenth in the period of time known in Latin as the *Pax Romana* or Roman peace." (exerpt from first chapter)

The Apostle John: A Blessed Life takes a historical and philosophical look into the life and work of this son of Zebedee. Once a "son of thunder," John's spiritual journey led him to become the man called to write a special, personal account of the life of Jesus. This book guides the reader through the world in which John lived and the gospel, letters, and revelation tale written with divine direction and his unique perspective.

From his days fishing with his father and brother on the Sea of Galilee, to his travels with Jesus, and finally to his last days writing and sharing Christ's word in Ephesus, this apostle truly lived a blessed life.

Contact the author or visit www.omorepublishing.com for purchase.

LaVergne, TN USA
04 November 2010

203530LV00003B/4/P